The Best Poet You Know

-Vol. 2-

Collector's Item

By Rodney Dewayne

The Best Poet You Know
Volume 2
Collector's Item

By Rodney Dewayne

Acknowledgements

Everything that I am or ever hope to be would not or could not be made possible without the grace of God.

Dedicated with honor in memory of Dalante "Tay Wizzle" Williams

Wasn't ready for you to leave can you tell from the tears we cry.
Wasn't ready for you to leave can you tell from the tears in our eye.
-"The Family"

I thank you more than you will ever know while loving you more than I could ever show: "Toni and Warren Turner" "Darius Fennell" "Kandice Sherril" "Kendell Lee" "Casey Johnson" "Michael Fredrick"

Humbled and grateful to everyone who has given encouraging words reminding me of my greatness. Thank you for the wisdom, the advice, the concerns and the support that's offered out of admiration and unconditional love and to you who would sit and listen as I went on and on about my dreams...
Forever grateful for the love...
Forever grateful for the prayers...
Forever grateful for the opportunity.

The Best Poet You Know

-Vol. 2-

Collector's Item

Table of Content

Michelle Obama
Baby Mama
Mama Said
I'm David. Who's Goliath?
Without You
Everything but Mine
Stayed So Long
Tameka Starks
High Mountaiun, Deep Sea
Cool Off
A Greater Gain
Prettiness
Stronger Tomorrow
I Do Not Need
Wifey Material
Our Women
Crossed My Mind
Yourself
For Ya'll
Nothin
Grew Up
Black Queen
To Each His Own
Rich than Famous
Long Live C.T
Mrs. Michele Renee Yancey
Her Name is a Woman
Oscar Performance
Best To Do It
No Friend of Mine
Killer Youth
Andrea Ontario
Pretty Blue Eyes

RODNEY DEWAYNE
"BEST POET YOU KNOW"

Rodney Dewayne

The Best Poet You Know

RODNEY DEWAYNE

Praying Position

My father which art in heaven your son hasn't
really been putting forth his best

Became friends of evildoers, meddled in drugs,
cops came and so did another arrest

Many of my family, friends and fans those who
believed and supported me

Are beginning to have doubts and at this moment
they are not as proud of me

My son Debraylon and I haven't spoken and this
ignorance has been going on for months

I've let pride get in the way of calling him up sitting
down and having a nice lunch

Topping it off its been so many murders and deaths
around here to keep up with lately

That I feel at war with my own heart it just
continues to ache me

I am accepting full responsibility for my
circumstances and my conditions

Because it was I who gave Satan power of tiring my
hands and not allowing my knees to bow in praying
position

Empty Pockets

When thy strings began to come loose and all seems to fall apart

We're not knowing it comes to the light those things which are hidden in the dark

The schemes and plots in which we premeditated to take advantage of another man

Not for one second registered one thought the harm we cause our brother man

Its because of our own selfish ambition misleading us astray on the journey of greed

No discerning of signs warning us to apply brakes when drifting at a reckless speed

There are hopes of a better tomorrow but slowly they are slipping further and further away

Especially when our dreams abruptly abandon us only to have hearses or cop cars continuously drive us away

So standing in front of the world on a mountain top counting a million profit

Is irrelevant to God because if the spirit is bankrupt then the heart is an empty pocket

Incomplete Sentence

It's been a stressful life

but I must admit it's been a blessful life

I'm a history book filled with battles and wars

But on this soldier body no wounds and no scars

A lot of the times we fail to succeed

Because we're focused on self and not on what the team need

I'm trying to fulfill a destiny and serve a purpose

That clowning and joking I drops it off at the circus

I remember I used to wake up and hate mornings

Now its better days, peaceful nights and great mornings

Kortnie L. Johnson

A champ of champions, multi-record holder, gold medal after gold medal all she's ever done was win

Check the books this is nothing new she been queen of the track since way back when

Making it known all around the globe that the best in the world proudly represents Italy, Texas

Literally just walks off and leaves the so-called competition with the victory of margin being from LSU to Italy, Texas

Coming around that final stretch opening up with the acceleration of a hungry cheetah

Even the light of day knows it must be at its best when she's proven its almost impossible to beat her

I would not be one bit surprised that before I have completed writing this line

That both of her arms are not raised in victory celebrating her greatness crossing the finish line

A historical rocket takeoff that accomplishes her mission and fulfills her destiny at world record speed

When Philippians 4:13 is her scripture, *'doing all things through Christ who strengthens me'* what else does she need?

Incarceration

Allow me to escort you through the brick walls,
razor wire and steel floors of incarceration

Because you have been wrongly misinformed if you
heard anything of it being like a vacation

Around here it's stone crazy day and night and you
seldomly see smiling faces

Them fast approaching dreadful court dates keeps
us all stressed out wearing worried faces

Some call it rumble in the jungle it's truly a place of
constant danger

Finding rest takes mastering up the courage to close
your eyes and sleep amongst total strangers

Mail call is temporary relief but a breath of fresh air
if you're a recipient of pictures and letters

Nothing in the world is better not even commissary
than hopeful words from loved ones saying it gets
better

Unless you're told to roll it up because bail is paid
or time is served and you're going home

So basically when locked away out of sight, out of
mind this is what goes on

Struggles of a Father

I remember it clearly being a kid when the police came and took my father away

My faith in God must have been with him because I don't remember praying since that day

The strength and patience that it required my father was incarcerated for 15 years in a prison cell

And not too long after I was captured, chained and thrown into a similar cell

A continuous of cycle I left my son to cry them same exact tears I once did

Because there is nothing worse in this world than not having your father growing up as a kid

Eventually my father was freed and sent home to gather the years that he had lost

His adjusting to routines was rough but earned his promotion and once again he's the boss

My daddy, my pops, my teacher, my twin, my father is my hero

So keep your mouth closed and your hands to yourself because I love that negro

Other Side of the Bridge

Every night instead of prayer they submit the same
evil request that I die in my sleep

So I'm knowing that it kills them every morning
that I awake and rise to my feet

It's all meaningless the down talking and spitting on
my name during their conversation

Their reaching with long arms and wicked hands
but unsuccessful of laying one finger on my
salvation

There will be no touching or harming one hair on
my precious head

So I pay no attention and would never listen to what
she say/he say ever said

Accomplishing my mission, staying focused,
pushing forward, no looking back, no regrets

The secret to life when its hardest is rubbing your
hand across your forehead and wiping sweat

Because on the other side of that bridge its greeting
success and enjoying life

Being well mannered, humbled and grateful on
knees nightly before bed appreciating Christ

No Devil in Hell

It is truly God this feeling of Heaven I have even
with all Hell going on around me

Their player hating my purpose, envying my destiny
but jealousy will never tie and bound me

God continues to be good all of the time even with
all of the bad that's aimed my way

Why are you captured in rumors and gossip when
it's God who has the last say

I exited back streets took a higher road now they
detest the way I travel

Proud of who I've become can't say I miss the dead
ends and loose gravel

Not spotless or perfect wouldn't waste precious
time trying to convince you of any of that

I played in dirt and made mud but every cruel word
spoken of me not guilty of all of that

There are accommodations, benefits and rewards in
being Rodney Dewayne so naturally they seek my
place

But no devil in hell will steal my joy, take my faith
or worry the smile off of my face

Our Community

Allow me to speak just briefly while being brutally honest about our community

I have lived here forever but never have I enjoyed love, peace and unity

We went from being family to strangers and now a every man for himself battlefield

Filled with emotional and spiritual poverty it's difficult not being hopeless when surrounded by drug deals

In ignorance we are killing each other with murders and AIDs but even worse when it's suicide

This is no longer an epidemic we have foolishly begun our own genocide

How can we be proud of anything or call ourselves achievers when our children are losing?

Is there anyone from anywhere who can help me understand because this is a bit confusing

I deeply love my community and keeps it close to my heart

But it's imperative we make changes and as of right now, today, is a perfect time to start.

Mama & Dan-Dan

I wonder who recognized who and approached
introducing themselves first

Regardless Dan-Dan you're now in the presence of
my Mama so you know you can't curse

But at the same time be yourself because Mama got
it how she lived

That even to this day all who knew her credit her
for being real

And Mama that's my loyal friend I often spoke of
who's name is tattooed on my left arm

Remember me saying when I cross paths with his
killer I'm causing him bodily harm

But that's for another time for now get to know one
another enjoy the meet and greet

I wrote a book in ya'll honor so when you look
down you'll be proud of seeing me shine in these
streets

Anyway I didn't want much just stopping by you
know how I do

Besides wouldn't pass up this opportunity to say
how much I miss and love both of you

It's All Political

Television sets across America are filled with
actors, entertainers and various leaders at war with
the President

While an epidemic of dead bodies continues to pile
sky high in my residence

Gods innocent and precious children left
unprotected victims of molestation with no safe
place to call home

With the predators being the parents who
themselves are products of dysfunctional homes

Voices screaming with outrage to a city council
whose seats are occupied with entirely white folks

Meaning our needs and concerns are comedy to
others who laugh at us like jokes

There are marches and rallies even riots and protest
up and down this chain of command

But until these privileged feet walk in poverty shoes
they will just never understand

So here it is the American way the poor gets poorer
as the rich get richer

Politics painted so beautiful by politicians that
20/20 vision seldom sees the ugly picture

Black History

Muhammad Ali: Floating like a butterfly and stinging like a bee in the middle of the ring.

Martin Luther King Jr. leading a march to the very place he first shared his legendary speech, 'I Have a Dream.'

Nelson Mandela: Being an extroadinary figure and example for the overcoming of life struggles and suffering for black men.

Tupac Shakur: Screaming thug life while jewelry flashing hanging out of the window of a 500 Benz.

Whitney Houston: As beautiful to the eyes as ears singing *The Greatest Love of All* just one last time.

Michael Jackson: Electrifying the stage and making it known worldwide why he is the greatest of all-time.

Rosa Parks: Raising hell at the front of the bus until equality and justice starts and racism stops.

The Notorious BIG: Being a Bad Boy, rocking Coogi, blessing the microphone putting on for Hip Hop.

Maya Angelou: Bringing peace, hope and humility in a prophetic pattern with spiritual gifts and healing words.

Malcolm X: Being bold and courageous, uncompromising and defiant by any means necessary and meaning every word.

Strength

A toddler for the first time beginning to walk who falls, gets up with no fear and tries again.

Or the boxer who was knocked down but recovers and in that same round gets the knock-out and wins.

A single mother with three kids, more bills when storms come her head stays above water.

Rent due with a car note two dimes one nickel never been short one quarter.

The visionary who gets up early mornings ridiculed and laughed at for pursueing a dream.

No support or encouragement from family or friends just a coaches congratulations for making the team.

The innocent who's beatdown and kicked, convicted before trial and treated so pig pen filthy.

Fallen to knees as tears hitting floor, screaming praises to God when juror comes back with verdict not guilty.

Blood, wounds and yellow tape being described as a horror scene from the depths of hell.

A clinging to life, a defying the odds, a miracle in which one lives to tell.

Young Black Males

We have accomplished everything up under the sun except the simple task of stopping to think.

With the epidemic of us murdered and suicides at this alarming rate pretty soon we will be extinct.

If this was a game to be played like a sport we would be losing with heads down embarrased because of our stats.

Across America cemetaries and prisons are filled over capacity and overwhelmly dominated by the color of black.

We are still single handedly turning our own beautiful black queens into fed up single mothers.

And then have the audacity to turn around being deadbeats and disrespect our baby mothers.

Since such a sensitive subject I will stray away from that conversation of the much needed child support.

And sweep around my own front porch and leave that headache to the courts.

I wish I could close my eyes and make believe but this is no happy ending fairytale.

Just a harsh reality that's easily captioned the struggles and hardships of us young black males.

Houses

Me and my brothers often expressed big dreams of someday organizing a power house.

But without proper structure and foundation dreams die fast meaning we grew up without a father in our house.

Greeted with disappointments and now knowing I'm eliminated from shaking hands with the president in the white house.

So there I was with no ambition, no goals and no graduation because I dropped out the school house,

And from then on I did nothing all day except wasted time hanging around at my neighbors house.

From there it didn't take long before I was risking it all being self-destructive in the drug house.

A lifestyle that drastically changed I was smoking weed and drinking liquor every weekend at the club house,

And in a bling of an eye I was standing handcuffed in front of a judge in a court house.

There was no money for lawyer and judge had no use for me I was escorted away to a jail house.

But now days I'm thanking God for his mercy and grace at the altar of the church house.

Instagram

I never envisioned losing my religion to something so simple as looking at a picture.

Until Instagram had me tongue kissing the screen of my cell phone literally trying to taste her picture.

There I stood looking a damn shame with a wet mouth like a baby drooling.

It's a man's world but a woman's kingdom and with that sex appeal she's ruling.

All she thinks of me is being a bug-a-boo as much as I'm in her DM.

And I'm often there, you can find me there from the AM to the PM.

It's just something magical about her make-up and hairdo, the way she styles herself.

Down to her outfits even the ones that don't fit the way she profiles herself.

It's fair to say I love her without meeting her it's just the way I am

But say what you want about me but you better not lay a finger on my Instagram.

Rodney DeWayne
"Best Poet You Know"

When I Pray

When I pray I pray our father which art in Heaven hallowed be thy name.

When I pray I pray for necessities of bread and water and not the luxuries of fortune and fame.

When I pray I pray for patience, understanding, wisdom and knowledge.

When I pray I pray our children abandon the school shootings graduate and soar off to college.

When I pray I pray for smiles, laughter, happiness, peace and joy by the bunch.

When I play I pray that someday Linda Gene and I are above our differences and sits down to enjoy lunch.

When I pray I pray from the heart with my entire mind, body and soul.

When I pray I pray for those who gains the world but loses their soul

When I pray I pray we are not led into temptation but believed from all evil.

When I pray I pray for the world, the future, mankind, sisterhood better days and a better people.

Product of My Environment

I'm being exactly everything that you made me.

Which is the absolutely nothing that you gave me.

Whether I was right or wrong went left of right you judged me.

Who knows what might have been if you would of loved me.

Who can survive when around every corner the streets are heartless.

With churches on every block but no trace of love or forgiveness because they are Godless.

The children are suffering, the youth are killers and elders are hateful.

God's judgement is here, his wrath upon us for our acts being of ungrateful.

This is no attempt to bash my community but there is no denying it.

So whether I swim, I drown or perish I'm the product of my environment.

This is For

This is for those that get up every morning and go hard single super mothers.

I see you representing worldwide and just had to let you know I love ya.

This one is for the women hustlers that's locked away in the feds and the state.

My independent bosses prospering without a man getting it in state to state.

This is for them ambitious women that's accomplishing every goal and reaching dreams.

The world is yours baby, girl go get it, royalties for the queen.

This is for the divas, the women beasting in life with hearts of a lion

And so effortless with gorgeous smiles, flawless bodies and beautiful minds.

But the unsung heros are those women resting peacefully with headstones and flowers on their graves.

Our gone but not forgotten who paved the way, extroadinary examples of living courageous and dying brave.

Follow the Leader

In the book of Exodus they had the great Moses but today look at our leaders.

So disqualified with blind vision and cowardly where besides another 40 years in the wilderness could they lead us.

How could they uplift with no strength or give hope to the people when they crumble themselves.

Our needs and concerns are tired of the deaf ears and blind eyes while they receive bribes under tables only helping themselves.

There is a God who sits high and looks low and is very displeased with his people.

Soon to expose the wolves in sheep clothing up rooting trees bearing no fruit with no patience for evil.

Collection plates are filled but there are no healing, blessings or miracles now don't that seem odd.

Of course it does because this material world praises money and no longer the greatness of God.

So go right ahead and stone me to death for being Matthew 7:16 judgemental

When in reality I'm just being brutally honest and leaving it to your leaders to be sentimental.

Amazing Grace

As eggs scrambled and bacon sizzled I would watch grandmother stand over the stove and say, "Amazing Grace, Amazing Grace."

How could I ever forget the memory of her with the joyful look on her face as she sang, "Amazing Grace, Amazing Grace."

The table set, plates prepared, heads bowed and before anyone savored the delicious taste, "Amazing Grace, Amazing Grace."

She piled my plate until my stomach was full making one wonder if I've eaten in days, "Amazing Grace, Amazing Grace."

Once excused from the kitchen it was déjà vu as she washed, dried and put dishes away, "Amazing Graze, Amazing Grace."

Then from behind her bedroom walls while getting ready for church she greatly loved that place, "Amazing Grace, Amazing Grace."

Even when in the car fastening the seat belts making sure we were safe, "Amazing Grace, Amazing Grace."

Up in church front row, hands raised, shouting, praising God, tears streaming down her face, "Amazing Grace, Amazing Grace."

Back home reclining in her favorite chair rocking back and forth I would hear her pray, "Amazing Grace, Amazing Grace."

Even today from the grave her resting place I can still hear my grandmother voice singing, "Amazing Grace, Amazing Grace."

Better Days

I do not post statuses being a member of a gang, I'm not cussing and shooting up the world.

I'm standing on and dying for morals and principals a hopeful future for our boys and girls.

To give them equal opportunities to run free unlocking every goal and dream.

Sitting them down with open books of untold stories from Mother Teresa to Martin Luther King.

So they can one day themselves open closed doors and windows wide.

Applying them with tools they can use that change the world while embracing humility and rejecting pride.

So with you spreading rumors, finger pointing and judging me, ask yourself what contributions have you made?

It's countless and documented all the single mothers in the community bills that I have paid.

So everyday you see me trust and believe I'm out here really trying to become something.

The whole community isnt just out here running up screaming my name giving me hugs for nothing...

Linda Guinyard

The forgiving of myself has been mountain moving impossible for my killing of two birds with one stone.

In an act of pure hatefulness not only did I break your heart but I broke my own.

I could go back and forth with the when and the why's but no excuses are accepted.

Truth of the matter God placed an angel in my life and I failed to acknowledge and respect it.

I have no memory of the last time we've spoken and only on old pictures have I seen you.

Unless I count the many times I've closed my eyes and dreamed of you.

In all of my ways I was unfaithful with pre-meditated broken promises taking full advantage of our friendship.

Now missing your beautiful presence and graceful essence all of the valuables that were overlooked in our relationship.

Now I'm just known as the guy who had it won but let his championship slip away

And as long as I live I'm forced to face the reality of these consequences everyday.

Wedding Ring

From just her simple touch she has me like a volcano ready to erupt.

This is a love affair that no family, friends or outsides will dare to interrupt.

Since she entered my life it has went from rainy days to sunshine, she's changed the weather.

And I'm not speaking of intercourse when I say that she loves me better.

In me she's found a diamond in the rough, in her I've found a best friend.

Who's helped me up, dust me off and made me feel like a man again.

So when in public we hold hands and in front of haters we tongue kiss.

Flying with cupid so high on cloud nine that we can't hear your diss.

I'd admit I'm sprung with nose wide open cause baby does her thing.

Got me at the jewelry store skipping lines with my last dollars because baby girl has earned herself a wedding ring.

Good Girl

She politely interrupted my conversation to inform me
that she has a man

and since first things are first she was making sure that I
understand

that he is the love of her life and together they share a
happy home.

So it would be disrespectful to him if she gave me the
number to her phone

I replied this would be between me and you and he
would never know.

Her response was sure he would because it's her place to
tell him so

because she's prayed and worked too hard on the
relationshop to just throw it away

and with that she gave a kind smile as she turned and
walked away.

I felt a small disappointment but no love lost because
she's a good girl

and truth of the matter we need more of them in this
unfaithful world.

Your Last Man

He was immature with the mindset of kids and played lots of games

used abusive language, showed no respect and called you humiliating names

throughout the relationship he cheated with girls who were less than you.

He was never supportive, but always challenging and testing you.

A no-show when you needed to be held, kissed and comforted on your worst day.

It fell on the same date every year but still he forgot your birthday again

and again every month he left you with all the bills.

Tries turning it around and blaming you when telling him how you feel.

This is not to belittle or throw salt on your last man

but to applaud you for finally waking up and throwing him in the trash can.

You Need

You need a man who remains confident knowing he has a strong woman.

You need a superman who fully trusts and believes in his superwoman.

You need a man who gives you the time, affection and attention your desires deserve.

You need a man who worships your whole body, every single bump, every single curve.

You need a man who cannot just lead and hold but also listen during a conversation.

You need a man who doesn't panic no matter the issue, problem or the situation.

You need a man that's above and beyond with a career, goals and dreams.

You need a man that first hands makes it known that you are his queen.

You need a man that any lucky woman would love to have.

You need a man that wouldn't trade you for the world because it's you he'd rather have.

If God Were a Woman

It would be done on earth as it is in Heaven.

There would be no acknowledgment of hate just a brilliance of love radiating twenty-four seven.

We would not be harassed with the hassle of politics and presidents.

There would be an abundance of patience and long suffering that structures and uplift our residents.

Mother nature would be respected, honored not bullied and dominated by mankind.

We would be raised as ladies and gentlemen with dignity not a history of manipulation and lying.

We would be awakened to great mornings with brighter days, longer nights with bigger stars.

A tomorrow that welcomes us with gratitude and respect because as a world we've come so far.

We would all live happily and forever underneath her providing and protecting wings.

There would be no conversations of race because we're all her children both kings and queens.

Some Say

Some say I dropped the bomb on her,

the way I blew her mind when I dropped the charm on her.

Some say that I took her race car fast,

calling it money in the bank swearing I can sit back and laugh.

Some say I got her completely head over heels,

I can do no wrong she's going nowhere just spinning her wheels.

Some say since I entered her life she hasn't been quite the same,

she is a totally different person everything about her has changed.

Some say that I am one of a kind,

with rare virtues and qualities that are hard to find.

Ten Roses

The first rose is me being nothing more than a gentleman on our first date.

The second rose is for how time flies when having fun and keeping you out late.

The third rose is to clarify your worth and I enjoyed your time.

The fourth rose indicates I'm so into you and wants all of your time.

The fifth rose is just because let's call it a gift.

The sixth rose is because I found someone who I can trust at the edge of a cliff.

The seventh rose is to puff you up with hopes you bestow me a kiss.

The eighth rose is for not just being the answer to every prayer but for fulfilling my wish.

The ninth rose suggests that I want more of your affection and more of your hugs.

The tenth rose is for the beginning of friendship and the beginning of love.

No Equal

Your rareness only comes once in a lifetime you have no equal.

Your presence cant be duplicated or reproduced there will be no sequel.

You are none other than an angel in human form such a Goddess

And I speak with total truth I'm not exaggerating I'm being modest.

When suggesting that your picture be displayed in the dictionary next to beauty.

Because on a bad hair day without a touch of makeup you're still a cutie.

Seeking but never finding anyone throughout the land nor around the world who compare.

From the men that admire you to the women who envy look how the eyes stare.

One by one they all fall short when standing next to you

They will have to be attached to greatness because even their best won't do

Michelle Obama

I dream of a fantasy that's being more than just
mediocre and residential

So its campaigning for that Democratic someone
who suits me up and makes me presidential

A woman of class that teaches me focus and keeps
my mind on things of value

A beauty of a woman that I will never get tired of
telling "I'm so lucky to have you"

And if I had to describe her in three words they
would be "I'm so impressed"

Not only is she instrumental in my growth and
achievements but has her own success

Someone I'll be proud to call wifey that's a mother
to my children and raises them well

Someone gentle and tender I can build with but still
possess the strength to hammer the nail

Then she's right there beautifully smiling and being
very encouraging after a long day

Being my shoulder to cry on and that angel of a
reminder to always pray.

Congratulations!

500 and Counting Sold of

The Best Poet You Know

By Rodney Dewayne

Baby Mama

Though it seems like forever and a day I'll never forget you being my girlfriend

The specific way you kissed and hugged me, had me thanking God for you again and again

Ask around a player with plenty women but she's the only one I ever fought for

So it doesn't take Einstein or two brains to know what I thought of her

I enjoyed the labor my pleasure putting the work in until the job was done

She hated me using condoms but loved when I used my tongue

It wasn't always a relationship built on cookies and cream we had our ups and downs

Just like any other relationship just refused to let it tear us down

So much that even to this day my homeboys still give me drama,

For not being able to say no when she call to my Baby Mama…

Mama Said

Mama Said: Thank God it's food on the table and the rent is paid

Be careful who you trust and love because betrayal can cut deeper than a razor blade.

Mama Said: Everyone that smiles in your face is not your friend

Some lessons are complicated so some teachings you will have to be taught again.

Mama Said: You had them so love and make sure that you take care of my grandkids

Whatever the cost be there for them no matter how small or how big.

Mama Said: I didn't raise you rich but I raised you well

You could be thrown in the ocean and not drown but set sail.

Mama Said: Before she died it's your life son live it however

Then she took her final breath, closed her eyes, and went to Heaven.

I'm David. Who's Goliath?

When I'm up I feel like a ladder the way I'm climbed on

When I'm down I feel like a circus the way I'm clowned on

But I don't cry over spilled milk I just get another cup and pour another glass

Trusting and believing in God's word that this too shall pass

So whether I'm wiping sweat from my forehead or blood from my nose

From through the crack in the concrete the dirtiest of circumstances with thorns and all I rose

Now they either hate, jealous or mad and I know exactly what their reason is

It's because I don't even care to acknowledge what their reason is

Not even the Giant Goliath could force me to curl up like a cat in a blizzard

I'm more Proverbs 30:28 in kings palaces with company of great men like the lizard…

Without You

I'm confirming and making it known that I did it without you

All because you never pictured me flying sky-high without you

Avoiding the slippery slopes while climbing mountain-high without you

I accomplished, achieved, and succeeded without you

Prospered and attained all the things I desired and needed without you

I smiled, laughed, enjoyed and found peace without you

While you were thinking I wouldn't survive and would be deceased without you

But instead I realized my true potential of what I could be without you

On a new path and my journey now is living life without you

With my final thought being I won't think twice about you.

Everything But Mine

When I can no longer trust and believe you

I'm slamming the door behind me as I leave you

You were being inconsiderate in public when you shamed me

Now you're being selfish turning it around trying to blame me

I have granted you the many things most women would die for

So I'm asking you again what was the lie for

Sometimes it's a hard job but we could have worked it out

We could have found a solution we could have searched it out

But you have went beyond boundaries and crossed the line

Put yourself in a position to be called everything, everything but mine.

Stayed So Long

To this day I'm still questioning? How could I have done such a horrible thing?

To have caused you to slip it off your finger and trash your engagement ring.

Hurriedly packed up your bags and ran as fast as you could out of the door.

All the proof I needed confirming that you didn't wanna hear it anymore.

In one ear out of the other your words of wisdom advising me to humble myself

Before it's too late and by the hands of my own I crumble myself

I was being both arrogant and ignorant and it made me cocky

But now I'm stressed out because this love affair is a little bit rocky

Brought into clear view that there is no sunshine when she is gone

And in all honesty I'm still shocked that you hung around and stayed so long.

Tameka Starks

I remember this one cold winter I was homeless and had no friends

Then appeared an angel who opened the doors to her heart and home and invited me in

At the time I was stingy with my feelings but that meant the whole world to me

Meanwhile in my heart there blossomed a love for you that will outlast eternity

I wrote this as tears formed in my eyes sitting in a jail cell

I can't thank you enough for being Heaven when everyone else showed me Hell

I still recall that conversation of me saying how I was going to win for you

Both grateful and humble you reversed it. Saying naw, you gotta win for you

So when I trip in life, stumble or fall I pray you still see it's all for the good

No excuse, but it's not the easiest thing being in a bucket full of crabs trying to climb out of the hood

But here is one promise I will never break, Rodney Dewayne is going to do his best

Fall to his knees every night showing appreciation for you and his blessings and letting God do the rest...

High Mountain, Deep Sea

I received a phone call from a good friend saying he was tired of crying

Tired of the murders, tired of death, tired of suicides, tired of the dying.

He was so emotional that all I could do was stand paralyzed and feel his pain

With compassion accompanying I sent prayers to God asking to cover him in Jesus name

As I searched throughout my heart seeking the words that could bring him hope

It was easy to discern he was hurting and weary and not far from the end of his rope

Then he replied that everyone was gone or leaving and no one was left but us

I digested his truth then responded have faith we've come a long way from back of the bus

But still I know he was right because every other week it's funerals and obituaries

And there are no words to make sense of any of it even if reading from dictionaries…

Cool Off

I'm dialing your number while hoping that you please answer the phone

And forgive me for being selfish because I know that I was wrong

I allowed immaturity and emotions to get the best of me

Now I'm feeling regrets and shame for allowing you to see less of me

I admit I don't know where to go or what to do next

That's the reasoning for blowing up your phone and sending back to back texts

Common sense tells me that you're angry and do not won't me to call again

But we both know me walking without you only means I'm falling again

Next time I stick my foot in my mouth I'll be sure to take my shoes off

My batteries are low so I'm putting my phone on the charger giving you time to cool off.

A Greater Gain

I thank God for the few in my life who do love me

And beyond grateful for the series of things they go out
of their way and do for me

Because many never check to see if I'm still breathing or
even alive

And when I appear their looking spooked as if it's a
ghost in their eyes

This is no sad story about me crying a river about who
wasn't there

Nor me playing victim stance or throwing a pity party
about who doesn't care

But more about me being a conqueror who overcomes
all and every opposition

Turning into footstools what was once perceived to be a
form of competition

There wasn't any energy wasted on finger pointing
neither to complain

Because I knew if my strength endured to the end there
was a Greater Gain...

Prettiness

Adorable, captivating, poetic, heavenly, praiseworthy, compelling, golden, dreamy, a paradise, extravagant, and classical not absurd.

Because when defining your remarkable beauty it requires using a multitude of pretty words.

Their pointing and whispering as if I'm out of my mind and not utilizing my brain.

But I must confess there's something about you so seductive that it knocks me off track like a derailed train.

With my hands holding a stack of Bibles I cross my heart and pledge not to lie.

From that very first moment that I saw you I had something that resembles love in my eye.

I'm both confident and adamant and know what I want when I see it.

Your glamorous smile that brightens the day like sunshine isn't a secret and should not be hid.

So advise and warn the world about this new guy who comes with a big crush.

And every time that he sees you it gives him a drug overdose type adrenaline rush.

Stronger Tomorrow

Because of today's injustice, pains and sorrow - I will be stronger tomorrow.

Because of my avoiding facts and truths that are hollow - I will be a better future tomorrow.

Because of my elders, experience, wisdom and knowledge I borrow - I will be undeniable tomorrow.

Because of the great examples both past and present I choose to follow - I will be a leader tomorrow.

I Do Not Need

You must have heard incorrectly because I do not need friends.

I have sons to father; I'm trying to raise men.

I do not get lonely; I do not need buddies.

I roam in the presence of women; I do not need cuddies.

I am antisocial with my business; I do not need the company of homeboys.

Because too many times in my life I have been loyal to the wrong boys.

My family is my entourage; I do not need cliques,

That would be quite foolish, ignorant, and illiterate.

I hold my own, I do not need the reassurance of a gang.

I stand tall alone, I am Rodney Dewayne.

Wifey Material

I knew that once I got my hands on you I was never taking them off

And that you would need the knives, the scissors, something to literally cut them off.

I love you in a manner that's easily perceived as me having two hearts.

So, when it comes to catering you with passion and ecstasy that's the easy part.

I live and die to be the man of your dreams while desiring my wife to be.

If not praising and praying to God then boasting and bragging about me.

Should I just pull the curtains back and give you a clear view

Contagious spirit, infectious laugh that holds no punches when proving her point of view.

Their attraction is shown through catcalls because you are disobedient and so bad in the physical.

My admiration is granted because I honor your righteousness and the fact that you are God fearing in the spiritual.

Our Women

From within our inner being we must manufacture a desire that whole heartedly loves them.

From high mountains to deep oceans one must go above and beyond for them.

Admire, appreciate, honor, encourage, inspire, bless, and respect them.

Go against the grain, out of our way, break our necks for them.

Make them our flowers, jewels, gems, pearls, pride and joy, treasure them.

Celebrate, delight in, worship as our queens, paradise pleasure them.

We should be embracing them with faithfulness, honesty, authenticity, it's obvious they deserve our loyalty.

Such amazing and graceful creatures, the fruit that God produced, nothing less than royalty.

Our women are in the mercy of our hands but will we build or tear down?

I, personally greed their presence, their laughter, their essence, smiling with their hair down.

Crossed My Mind

It never ever crossed my mind,

that after a pleasant childhood comes an adulthood that is so unkind.

It never ever crossed my mind,

that there would be days of repeated rain causing the sun to retract it's shine.

It never ever crossed my mind,

that loving and trusting you would backfire with results of betrayal and lying.

It never ever crossed my mind,

that I would ever be handcuffed and shackled, locked away doing time.

It never ever crossed my mind,

that death would occur and I'll be seeing you for the last time.

RODNEY DEWAYNE

THE BEST POET YOU KNOW

RODNEY DEWAYNE

THE BEST POET YOU KNOW

FROM CLASSIC TO MASTERPIECE

Yourself

Love yourself

By going above and beyond yourself

Be proud of yourself

By not following crowds doing it yourself

Help yourself

By protecting yourself

Better your health

By educating yourself

Stop playing with yourself

And start praying for yourself

For Ya'll

I know I let a few of yall down a time or two

But if it means anything I'm truly sorry for what I put you through

Out of nowhere this life of mine took a turn for the worse

It's either Heaven blesses you or Hell curse

I could give you excuses until your head would spin

Or just give you my word and not do it again

If the attack comes physically I'm just have to fight harder

If the attack comes mentally I'm just have to think smarter

So whatever the opposition that confronts me in the future I'm give my all

No longer being selfish so I'm do it for y'all

Nothin

They called me broke when I had nothin'.

They laughed at me when I had nothin'.

They talked about me when I had nothin'.

They whispered about me when I had nothin'.

They pointed at me when I had nothin'.

They denied me when I had nothin'.

They put me down when I had nothin'.

They ignored me when I had nothin'.

They made jokes when I had nothin'.

But tables turn and now they hands out and I don't have nothin'.

Grew Up

I'm told I'm seasoned and quite wise for my young years,

but those lessons were not easily taught through a long history of many tears.

I owe a large portion of my proceeds to being self-motivated,

because without him being there keeping me encouraged I would have never made it.

I have set a high expectation for myself of being great.

Bread, meat, vegetables, and dessert, everything on the plate.

And it's all because of hard work I did not luck-up

I was down to nothing until I chose to look-up.

There comes a time in life when we will have to grow up.

I took responsibility for myself and my actions, matured and grew up.

Black Queen

Its God given and my voice is that awareness that
they can never copy your style.

Your physique is matchless and there is no other
beauty that compares to your smile.

Your unwarranted struggles and long suffering have
equipped, prepared and made you stronger.

Created for a golden purpose with a resilient spirit
and a tasteful hunger.

And I know that we sometimes disappoint and
performs less than kings

but you have never once denied loving and
understanding us as human beings.

Your boldness, capacity, influence, contributions,
intellect, nature, character, leadership, and authority
is Paramount.

Your attributes are wholesome, fruitful, poetic,
universal, and elegant with goodness and each and
everyone count.

Just your confidence alone makes it impossible not
feeling inferior to you.

Up under the Heavens there is not a soul, creation,
or invention superior to you.

To Each His Own

One of the hidden secrets of life is there must be an attitude of persistence.

A bold and confident mouth that speaks the impossible into existence.

A champion of a heart that battles and wars everyday being undefeated.

A mentality both firmly planted and deeply rooted with a perseverance that's never deleted.

A humility that puts down the pride and becomes proud of ourselves.

Because it's all futile if we fail to love thy neighbor as we love ourselves.

I envision a walk so stylish and fashionable it's Taylor-Made.

With the designer being faithful and entrusting of God to lead the way.

The obedience of these commandments will secure you an eternal appointment,

Or be the one who has it all under the sun and still dies in disappointment.

Rich Than Famous

I never wanted to be rich and famous

I wanted to be more rich than famous

I wanted to do great for my people and make my mother proud

Be my father's pride and joy and the reason he laughs loud

Being positive and productive doing good with bad circumstances

Show how extremely thankful and grateful I am for being given second chances

Make the most of countless opportunities from another day I wasn't promised

So I will rejoice, I will cherish it, I promise

I never wanted to be rich and famous

I wanted to be more rich than famous

Long Live C.T

In just a split of a second, A blink of an eye you were gone and took our hearts away...

Knowing that the future is without your smile and laughter only makes it a harder day...

In one way, form or fashion you loved, inspired or motivated us all...

So you can only imagine the devastation thats occurring in our hearts seeing our hero fall...

Its one of them life changing moments that the reality of the mind will never believe...

Crying out from the depths of the soul could you please come back we were not ready for you to leave...

Your city of Hilltop responded with pure love if you were here you would feel like a superstar...

A belated and deserving appreciation for all the dark nights that you were our bright and shining star...

We must learn to accept that sometimes what we yearn is not what is meant to be...

The only guarantees that comes with a promise is that hard work pays off and long live C.T...

Mrs. Michele Renee Yancey

I love and treasure many but there is none in this lifetime more sacred or as important to me…

Without your obedience to God in my past praying for my future then today where would I be…

Your focus was never on where I come from or what I've done…

Just a whole bunch of loving me like a mother loves a son…

It's easy knowledge why the spirits of death, disease and handicaps ran from me…

Because I'm beyond blessed and fortunate to have such a beautiful angel praying for me…

If asked what makes you great I would have to answer your consistence…

To instill in me never to apart from God's word and to speak my greatness into existence…

Now bullying with a faith that believes that any minute it could be my hour…

For not being uprooted by the weeds but instead blossoming as a flower…

Her Name Is A Woman

If men could have alone accomplished great things,
multiplied and expanded the earth why did God
create a woman

Therefore we must alleviate from discrediting,
taking from, hindering, and distrusting a woman

We should be eagerly thankful for a woman while
showing more gratitude and healing towards a
woman

Life would not be properly nourished, matured and
birthed without the labor and long suffering of a
woman

Not a day goes by that I don't try to fall in love with
a woman

In the first book of Genesis she was given a rib but
now its time to give our heart to a woman

My greatest joy has always been conversating and
laughing while being in the presence of a woman

Who would I be as a man if my mother,
grandmother and aunties were not a woman

My strongest prayer is that my sister and nieces
mature into the luxury, beauty, and essence of a
woman

It could never be repaid all of the wisdom and knowledge, valuable lessons learned through the experience of a woman

Oscar Performance

This is not a walking away or saying good-bye just
ascending to a higher level

And may I add so beautifully, courageously,
sophisticated and deserving of every medal

Telephones of in need, broken and battered are
ringing at alarming rates answer your calling

Which is to capture with hands of sympathy the
unbalanced, stumbling and falling

And if God were a woman she would be made in
the image of you

With your nature and your design it's not by
coincidence we praise every inch of you

When their looking sideways and talking with
envious whispers don't you dare feel wrong

Just be reminded of your greatness and never
doubting that eagles fly alone

A fruitful life speaks for itself so continue diamond
shining, be blessed and prosper

Your performance has been one in a lifetime
Heaven awaits you with an Oscar.

Best To Do It

There is no disrespect intended towards Maya Angelou, Tupac Shakur, or none of them...

Frederick Douglass, Langston Hughes I got the up most respect for all of them...But I'm best to do it

Not to downplay Robert Frost, Edgar Allen Poe, or none of them...

William Shakespeare, Mother Theresa, I have a genuine love for all of them...But I'm best to do it

I have huge gratitude and kind words for The Great Alice Osward, Mark Twain and all of them...

Tashita Bibles, Mike Guinn are so inspirational I'm inspired by all of them...But I'm best to do it

There is absolutely nothing that can be taken away from Sister Soul Jah, Ralph Waldo Emerson or none of them...

Paul Lawrence Dunbar, Walter Mosely, paved the way true definition of pioneers all of them...But I'm best to do it

Such an honor to be recognized and held in high regards with so many iconic and influential names

But as for being the best poet you know that crown is worn by Rodney Dewayne...I'm best to do it

No Friend of Mine

No friend of mine would ever allow the fact that
I'm prospering and doing well to make them

vomiting sick, going out of their way purposely to
make my life hard as arithmetic.

No friend of mine would throw slugs, pebbles, or
stones at my shack, mansion or Glass House

or make laughter of my homelessness for when I
didn't have a house.

No friend of mine would dare eat in my face and
not offer a crumb off of his plate

how could you possibly love me when all you're
demonstrating is hate.

No friend of mine would notice me stumbling near
the edge and push just to see me tumble

never once cheered when I had the ball secretly
awaiting for me to fumble.

No friend of mine would ever snatch blankets and
covers to expose my nakedness for the world
to see

instead of sharing a relationship built on brotherly love and compassion it was founded on envy and indecency.

No friend of mine would smile in my face and quickly as I turned sabotage and destroy me behind my back

my mama always told me that a real friend would never do any of that...

Killer Youth

Sometimes the hurt is so difficult it crushes their
spirit because it doesn't comprehend the pain

In midst of their tragedy tears keep their face so wet
you'll think they live life standing in the rain

From broken and dysfunctional households where
kindness and compassion was never concerned with
what their suffering was

Only to have inexperienced teachers and false
preachers fail to reach the children who is indigent
of love

But now its an addiction because their twisted
minds and hopeless spirits need the drugs

But before you are too quick to judge where were
the open arms when they needed a hug

Remember it being man and wife now when I love
you and marry you its the same sex

Their society is that of Solomon and Gomorrah laws
passed permitting intercourse and orgies with same
gender, same sex

Now on the news every other week their walking up
in churches and schools with loaded AK's

And if its breathing they shooting, wounding, and
killing everything in their got damn way...

Andrea ♡ Ontario

No secret that I live life outspoken and surrounded by controversy but who dares to hit me...

Win lose or draw, war, battle or fight history shows Andrea and Ontario was always in the trenches with me...

A thorn arose my foolishness where I lacked understanding causing us to not quite see eye to eye...

Even then you sacrificed time and energy from your lives checking on mine making sure I was getting by...

I swear its been like a million times I was distressed at rock bottom you provided hope...

Mindful of my being fatigued grasping for strength barely holding on at the end of my rope...

On many nights and occasions I've let Heaven know who you are and about all the extra hearts that you given me...

Asking in return it opens and showers you with grace, beauty, and generosity all of the virtues that you've given me...

Never threw your towels in represented my efforts
and corner faithfully with encouragement...

Without you superheroes in my life I'd never
rescued myself your unconditional love is
monument...

Pretty Blue Eyes

I looked into the most pretty blue eyes that one could ever have imagined

That was complimented by a smile so graceful that it could have won a beauty pageant

I stood there frozen like a deer captured in headlights until she walked away

Then I bent over grasping for air that's how much she took my breath away

If not for the separation that was caused from my circumstance

I'll put a suit on, conduct myself as a gentleman and ask her to slow dance

I've found the cure to my sickness and all of a sudden I'm feeling well

Down on a knee asking if she would be my cinderella with the starring role in my fairy tale

With no disrespect intended just utilizing a lesson that was learned as a kid

If you want it the world is yours especially with the rare courage to dream big...

More to Come from The Best Poet You Know…

Made in the USA
Columbia, SC
21 November 2021